Published by Copper Publishing
NSW, Australia
www.copperandpebo.com
email:enquiries@copperandpebo.com
phone:1300 734 695
copyright © Jane Eldridge, 2007
Illustrated by Brooke Lewis

All rights reserved. Without limiting the rights under copyright reserved above, no part of this publication may be reproduced, stored in or introduced into a retrieval system or transmitted, in any form or by any means (electronic, mechanical, photocopying, recording or otherwise), without the prior written permission of the copyright owner of this book.

An Australian production. Design by Brooke Lewis
Printed in Australia by McPherson's Printing Group
National Library of Australia
Cataloguing-in-Publication Data

Eldridge, Jane
The Beach With No Sun
ISBN 978-0-646-45399-6

Dedication:
To Mum and Dad for taking us
on holidays to the beach
every single year.

Every day of the summer holidays, the same thing happened. Sea kids by the thousands flocked to Whitewash Beach to swim and play with the sun. This day was no different.

So, when the sun arrived to wake Copper the sea kid and Pebo his pup, the pair were already out of their beds and dressed, ready to go.

"We've been up for ages, Sun," chirped Copper, thrilled to see his best friend. "Where were you? Did you sleep in this morning?"

"Actually," replied Sun. "Moon forgot to wake me when she went to bed. So yes, I am running a bit late. I need to move quickly!"

"You sure do," said Copper. "You need to get yourself high up in the sky so you can start warming the waves and heating the sand. And remember," he added with a little squeal. "It's school holidays! Fun, fun, fun! Sea kids everywhere!"

Sun was still tired and less than enthusiastic about the prospect of another big day.

"How could I forget!" came the weary response. "I do the work of nine planets at this time of year! From melting ice blocks and rounding up the flies to warming chips for the seagulls. You're right my friend, I had better get moving."

Copper shivered with anticipation at the thought of him and Pebo skylarking in the surf. "You'll still have time for games won't you Sun?" he asked a little anxiously. "You know, after you've dried the washing?"

"Games? Did you say games, Copper sea kid? Fun and games are my most important job!" replied the sun. "Of course I'll have time for games! I'm off now. I'll get started on vitamin D production and then move straight through to filling the world with happiness. I should be high in the sky by about midday. Is that alright with you?"

Copper saluted. "Twelve midday sharp, Boss," he said, trying to look serious under his grin.

But something very shocking and scary was waiting for Copper and Pebo on Whitewash Beach at twelve midday.

There were no sandcastles, no beach towels and no buckets and spades. But worst of all there were no sea kids. There was nothing! Nothing but a very miserable Sun.

"What's going on, Sun?" asked a bamboozled Copper. "Where's all the fun gone? Where are the sea kids?"

"They've been rescued," whimpered Sun in a frail and broken little voice.

"The shark alarm again, Sun?" asked Copper excitedly. "Was there a rescue? Could you see a fin?"

Staring out to sea, Sun replied without even blinking.

"Not a shark alarm, my friend. A Sun alarm!"

Copper was confused. "A Sun alarm?" he asked. "What's a Sun alarm?"

Sun's voice quivered, choking back tears. "It's a warning for sea kids to stay away from the sun," came the timid response. "The sun if you please! Me!"

"But why?" asked Copper.

Hurt and ashamed, Sun's voice was weak and empty. "Sunburn," he mumbled so quietly that he could barely be heard.

"I beg your pardon, Sun?" said Copper, leaning closer to his miserable friend.

"I said sunburn", repeated Sun. And with that, the tear drops fell.

Sunburn was bad. Every sea kid knew that. Not only was it painful, it could hurt your eyes and damage your skin. And even worse, you could end up with skin cancer when you grew up.

"What can we do about it, Sun?" Copper asked gingerly, not really knowing what to say to a crying Sun.

"It's not we," said Sun, bravely. "It's you, my friends. You and Pebo will have to play with Moon instead of me. You'll have to go to the beach at night and play under the stars so you don't get sunburnt. You see, I'm most dangerous between ten in the morning and three in the afternoon and that..." said Sun, swallowing hard to keep from crying, "...that was our best time for games!"

Sun was right. That was their best time for games! When Copper imagined his mother saying 'turn off the television and go and play outside in the moonshine', it wasn't the same.

"But we want to play with *you*," said Copper. "Not Moon! Can't you just stop burning us?"

Sun thought long and hard before answering. And then, with one last burst of self control said, "Copper, my little friend, we have a problem – a big one. It seems there is a hole in the sky. You can't see this hole but it's there and it's letting through some of my very dangerous rays. In fact," said Sun, "It seems I've become a complete menace to the earth!"

And then buckets of tears fell so hard that Pebo thought it was raining.

"Can we fix the hole?" asked Copper.

"I suppose it's possible," said Sun in between sobs. "But it will take years! And until it's fixed I've got no one to play with! Everyone thinks I'm bad! I'm getting some really nasty coverage from the newspapers and I'm even on the six o'clock news! I'm dodging reporters left, right and centre! I don't mean to damage people's skin! It's not fair!"

Copper found himself in a very dicey predicament. On one hand, he wanted to stay at the beach to support his friend. But on the other hand, the longer he stayed with Sun, the more chance there was he'd get sunburnt.

So he started shovelling little handfuls of wet sand onto his feet and knees to keep them covered and safe from Sun's dangerous rays. He held the sand in place with seaweed that Pebo had fetched from the shoreline.

Sun was so caught up in troubles of an ultra violet nature that the antics of Copper and Pebo went completely unnoticed. So when Pebo bounded up to Copper with one last piece of seaweed, and Copper placed it on his head for a hat, Sun didn't notice.

But Copper's mind was ticking over. He had an idea.

"It's okay, Sun! I know what to do!" said Copper, convinced he'd solved the problem. "I can stay like this! If I'm covered in sand and seaweed your rays can't get me! That's the answer!"

Sun's face began to brighten up. "Do you think so?" Sun asked Copper hopefully, a little worried about the flies swarming around the sea kid's face.

"It could be," said Copper, distracted by the buzzing. "I might need to wash yesterday's ice cream off though. That would cut down on the flies I guess! Come on Pebo! Race you in!"

And with three big skips Copper and Pebo were cavorting in the surf, splashing each other with the frothy foam from the waves and washing off the sand and smelly seaweed.

The sea kid and his pup ducked under the dumpers and floated over the swell, giggling and gurgling big mouthfulls of the ocean.

When Copper finally surfaced on the beach side of an enormous dumper, he was back on the job.

"Hey Sun," he called to his friend, "I think I've got an even better idea! What if I stay in the water? That way I wouldn't have to wear the seaweed! The flies won't get me and neither will your dangerous rays! We can still play! I'll just make sure I'm covered by water! It's a brilliant idea! What do you say?"

Sun didn't react. "If only you were right, my friend," said Sun. "But that won't work either. My dangerous rays are actually reflected off the water, so the ocean, or any water for that matter is still a 'no go' zone."

Nodding in despair, Sun turned to Copper and added, "I'm afraid it's over, my friends. We've had some marvellous times and some great games, but now you will have to play with the moon for twenty years or so."

And with that, Sun disappeared behind the clouds.

But Copper wasn't put off so easily. "Sun*nn*! Sun?" he yelled breathlessly, tripping up the beach with Pebo in tow, barking madly.

"Don't worry! I've just thought of something! If you stay behind the clouds we can't get burnt! You stay on that side and we'll stay on this side! Perfect! We can still sort of play but not get burnt! Isn't that a great idea?"

Sun peeked back through the clouds still looking glum.

"Yes, I know it sounds like a good idea, Copper, but that won't work either," said Sun. "You see, the clouds only *scatter* my rays. To be honest with you, sometimes the sunburn is even *worse* on a cloudy day. Forget it. There's no solution to this problem. But thanks for trying so hard."

"Well just wait there for two more minutes," pleaded Copper. "Pebo's got one more idea and it's a beauty!" he said. "It's a surprise and *you are going to love it*! Now *close your eyes*," said Copper, reversing up the sand so he could check that Sun wasn't peeking.

Sun couldn't resist a game, and joined in the fun with tightly closed eyes.

With his head held high and grinning proudly, Copper bowed and then presented Pebo and his surprise to the waiting Sun.

It was the boldest, brightest brolly that Sun had ever seen on Whitewash Beach.

"I say, that is truly fabulous!" said Sun, who's mood had lifted considerably. "And what a magic idea! I have to agree, there's no way I could burn you through a *beach umbrella*! I think you've solved my problem, friends."

"And just wait until you see it in action!" said Copper proudly as he and Pebo darted back into the water with the brolly in full sail.

But it was a disaster! The umbrella was big and clumsy and Copper couldn't swim and hold it at the same time. Besides, Pebo almost drifted out to sea with it.

Sun blinked away a tear. No matter how hard they tried, the two friends couldn't find a solution. Sun disappeared back into the clouds.

Next morning, Sun was too upset to come out to play.
The rain came instead and delivered a message from Sun.

"You know, Pebo," said Copper to his hairy friend, "This is absolute frippery! There *must* be a way we can play with Sun without getting sunburnt. I mean, we're not safe in the water, and the clouds don't block out Sun's rays. The sand and seaweed *sort* of did, at least until we went into the water and they washed off! And the beach umbrella *definitely* worked! If only we could find one that screws into people's heads. That's it, Pebo! I've got it!" shouted Copper. "Let's get to the beach and find Sun."

"Can we play now, Sun?" asked Copper, bursting with pride and the anticipation of fun and games. "You can't burn us now because we've covered up. We're Sun safe! Do you like the look?"

And for the umpteenth time that summer holidays, Sun was speechless.

"Copper sea kid, you are a genius and a great friend," Sun eventually managed to say. "How did you come up with such a brilliant idea?"

"It was easy, Sun," said Copper. "You see, it's like this. The earth's got a problem, so you've got a problem. Right?" Sun nodded in agreement.

"Well, if you've got a problem, we've all got a problem because it's no fun on the beach without Sun. So, I figured that we need to work together to manage the hole in the sky. And that's simple! We cover up our bodies!"

"I see!" said Sun. "Wearing protective swimwear on the beach and in the water stops my harmful rays from getting to you. Is that right?"

"That's exactly right, Sun," said Copper. "As long as we remember to restrict our play time together to before ten in the morning and after three in the afternoon and we, apply plenty of sunscreen, we're sweet! What do you say, Sun?" asked Copper triumphantly.

With head held high, shoulders straight and nose pointed towards the sky, Sun's posture said it all.

"The world can love me again!" beamed Sun proudly. "I'm back where I belong! Fair plumb in the middle of fun!"

The End

Tips for staying sun safe

- Avoid the sun between 10 in the morning and 3 in the afternoon.

- Try to play in the shade whether you are in the water or not. Beach umbrellas and trees are great for shade

- Always wear a 50+ UPF (SPF) swim shirt in the water. Long sleeves are best and make sure the shirt has a high neck.

- Always wear a hat in the sun whether you are in the water or not. A wide brimmed hat is best and make sure the back of your neck is covered. A legionnaire style is perfect

- Make sure you put sunscreen on the parts of you that can see the sun. Always use a broad spectrum water resistant sunscreen with a UPF (SPF) rating of 30+.

- Remember your sunglasses! Wear a wrap around style that gives you a maximum protection from the sun's harmful rays.

And don't forget Sun is your friend!!

www.ingramcontent.com/pod-product-compliance
Lightning Source LLC
Chambersburg PA
CBHW060800090426
42736CB00002B/105